AI WORLD
AI IN SPACE

by Ford Chambers

pogo

Ideas for Parents and Teachers

Pogo Books let children practice reading informational text while introducing them to nonfiction features such as headings, labels, sidebars, maps, and diagrams, as well as a table of contents, glossary, and index.

Carefully leveled text with a strong photo match offers early fluent readers the support they need to succeed.

Before Reading

- "Walk" through the book and point out the various nonfiction features. Ask the student what purpose each feature serves.
- Look at the glossary together. Read and discuss the words.

Read the Book

- Have the child read the book independently.
- Invite them to list questions that arise from reading.

After Reading

- Discuss the child's questions. Talk about how they might find answers to those questions.
- Prompt the child to think more. Ask: Why do people use AI in space? What might AI help us discover next?

Pogo Books are published by Jump!
5357 Penn Avenue South
Minneapolis, MN 55419
www.jumplibrary.com

Copyright © 2025 Jump!
International copyright reserved in all countries.
No part of this book may be reproduced in any form without written permission from the publisher.

Library of Congress Cataloging-in-Publication Data

Names: Chambers, Ford, author.
Title: AI in space / by Ford Chambers.
Description: Minneapolis, MN: Jump!, Inc., 2025.
Series: AI world | Includes index.
Audience: Ages 7-10
Identifiers: LCCN 2024030331 (print)
LCCN 2024030332 (ebook)
ISBN 9798892135689 (hardcover)
ISBN 9798892135696 (paperback)
ISBN 9798892135702 (ebook)
Subjects: LCSH: Astronautics—Data processing—Juvenile literature. | Artificial intelligence—Technological innovations—Juvenile literature. Outer space—Exploration—Technological innovations—Juvenile literature.
Classification: LCC TL793 .M187 2025 (print)
LCC TL793 (ebook)
DDC 629.40285/63—dc23/eng/20240724
LC record available at https://lccn.loc.gov/2024030331
LC ebook record available at https://lccn.loc.gov/2024030332

Editor: Alyssa Sorenson
Designer: Emma Almgren-Bersie

Photo Credits: Dima Zel/Shutterstock, cover (top), 11; ixpert/Shutterstock, cover (bottom); santiago1012/Shutterstock, 1; Frame Stock Footage/Shutterstock, 3; Dima Zel/Shutterstock, 4; NASA, 5, 6-7, 12-13, 17, 20-21; Triff/Shutterstock, 8-9; Claudio Caridi/Shutterstock, 10; 24K-Production/iStock, 14-15; NASA/piemags/Alamy, 16; Lukasz Pawel Szczepanski/Shutterstock, 18-19; Temstock/Shutterstock, 23.

Printed in the United States of America at Corporate Graphics in North Mankato, Minnesota.

TABLE OF CONTENTS

CHAPTER 1
AI in Rovers 4

CHAPTER 2
Studying Space 10

CHAPTER 3
Future Space AI 16

ACTIVITIES & TOOLS
Try This! 22
Glossary 23
Index 24
To Learn More 24

CHAPTER 1
AI IN ROVERS

A **rover** drives on Mars. This **robot** studies the planet. Why? It helps us learn more about it!

The rover stops. It points a **laser** at a rock. It melts part of the rock. The rover studies what it is made of. How? It uses **artificial intelligence** (AI)!

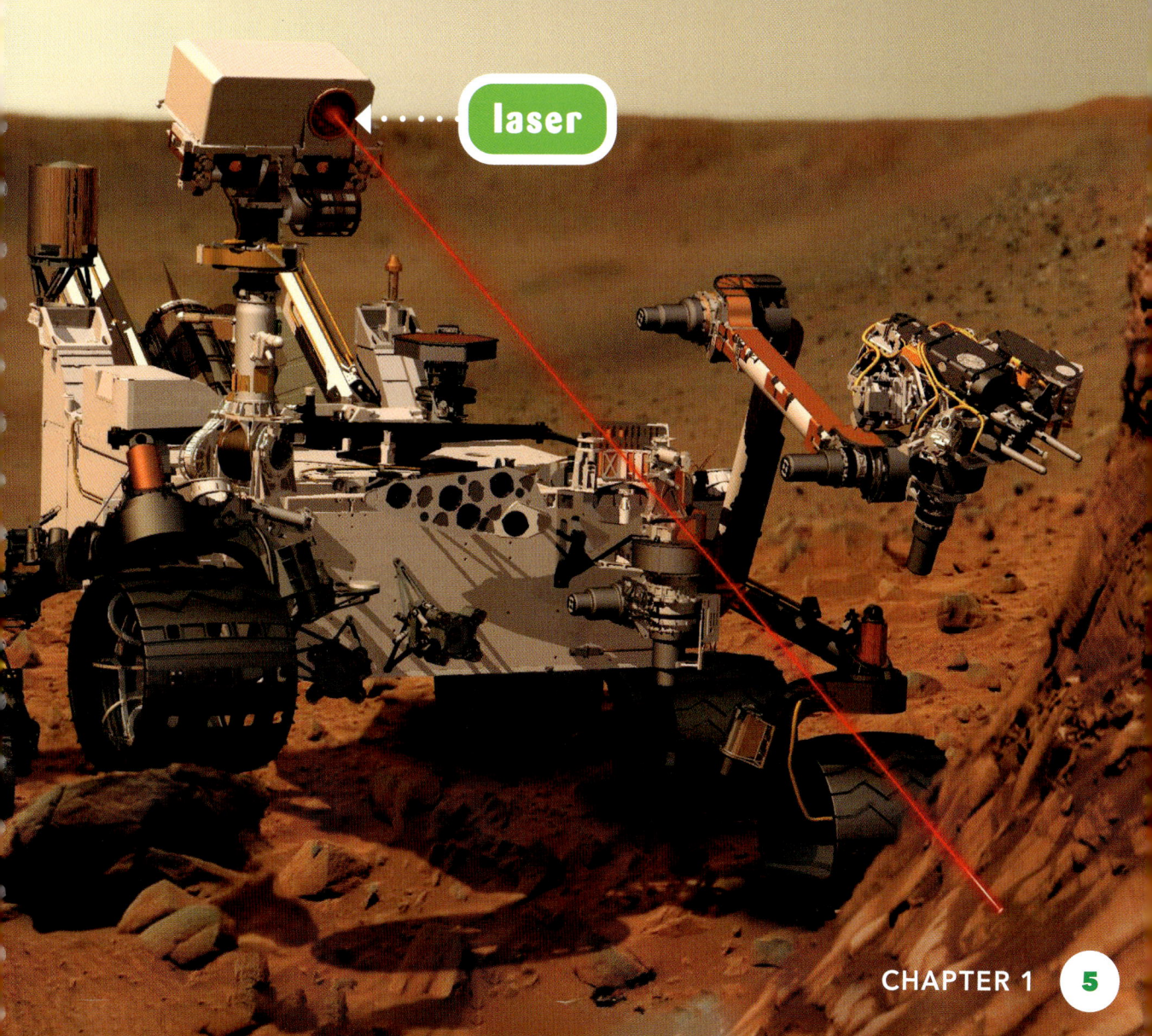

laser

CHAPTER 1 5

AI helps rovers do things humans use knowledge and skills to do. A rover has a computer. It has cameras and **sensors**. These send information to AI. Then AI makes decisions. Like what? It sees where large rocks are. It knows to drive around them. It finds more rocks to study.

TAKE A LOOK!

What are the parts of a rover? Take a look!

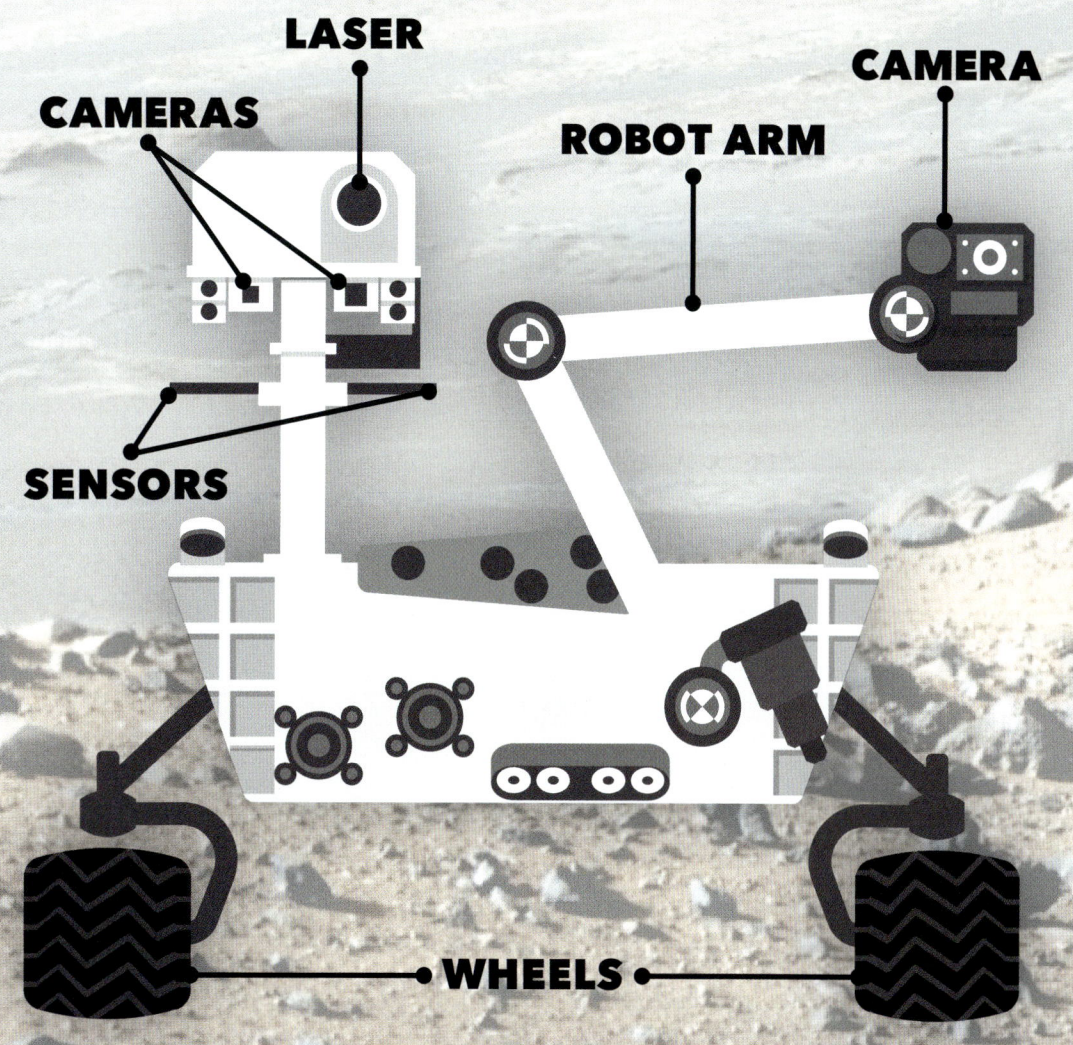

CHAPTER 1

Rocks tell scientists what the land used to be like. They show that Mars once had lakes. Water is needed for life! Was there life on Mars? Could living things be there now? Scientists are trying to find out.

Outer space is huge. Scientists use machines to gather **data**. AI studies it. It helps scientists learn about our universe.

DID YOU KNOW?

As of 2024, humans had never been to Mars. Scientists send rovers instead. Why? It is safer. We need to learn more about the planet before sending people.

CHAPTER 1

CHAPTER 2
STUDYING SPACE

Scientists have many questions. Is there life on other planets? Where is the safest spot to land on the Moon? How big is the universe? AI helps search for answers.

Moon

Astronauts live and work on a space station. It is a large **spacecraft**. It orbits Earth.

CHAPTER 2 — 11

Robots help astronauts. They carry objects. They record what happens on the space station. Why? People on Earth can make sure the spacecraft is OK. AI keeps the robots from bumping into walls and astronauts.

CHAPTER 2

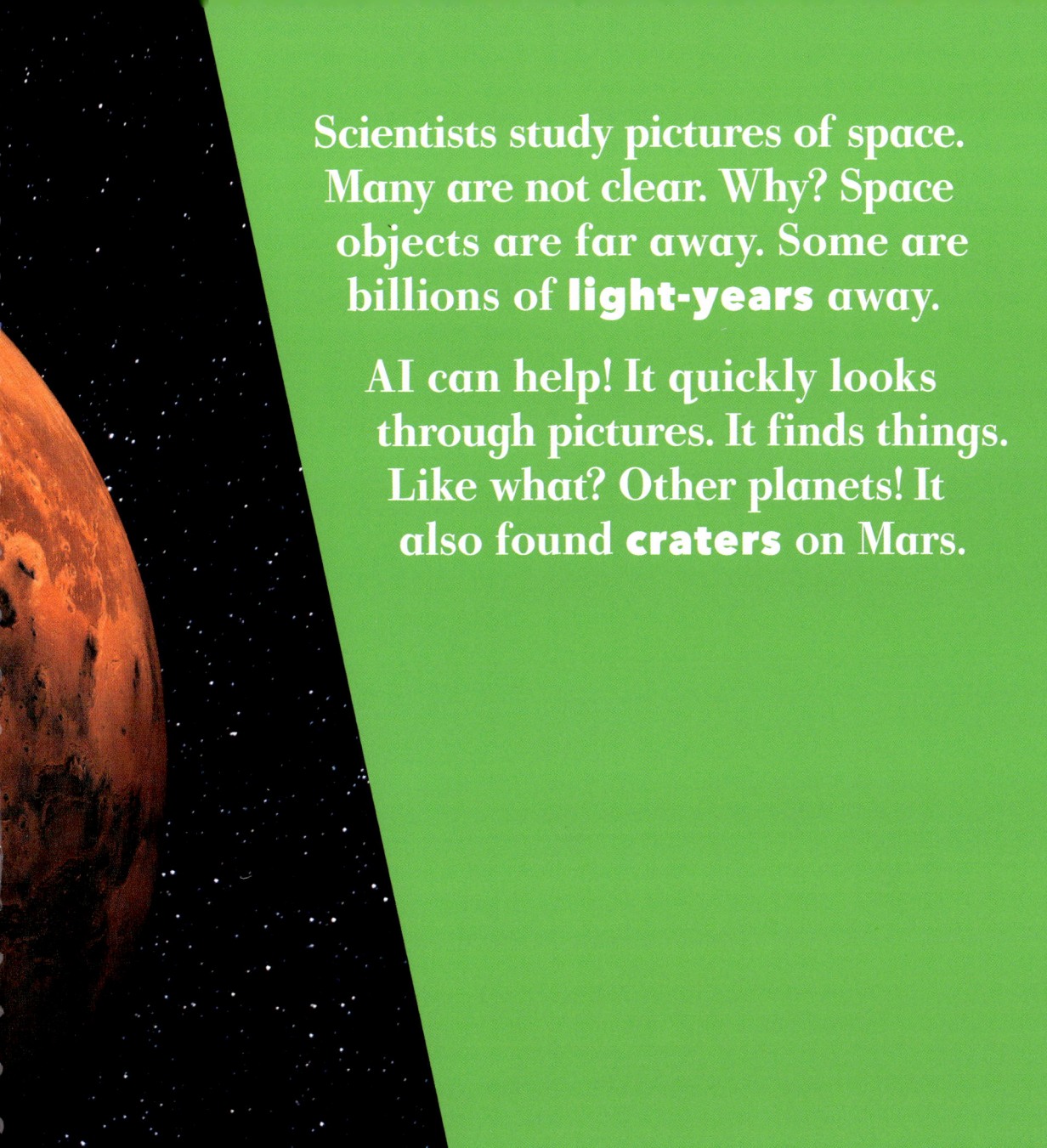

Scientists study pictures of space. Many are not clear. Why? Space objects are far away. Some are billions of **light-years** away.

AI can help! It quickly looks through pictures. It finds things. Like what? Other planets! It also found **craters** on Mars.

CHAPTER 3
FUTURE SPACE AI

> Scientists are building new rovers. As AI gets smarter, so will rovers.

Someday, robots could work outside spacecraft. Why is this important? Many things can go wrong in space. Astronauts could stay safe inside.

CHAPTER 3

AI could keep Earth safe. How? It could spot an **asteroid**. It could tell scientists. They would have a chance to stop it before it hit Earth.

> ### DID YOU KNOW?
>
> How might scientists stop an asteroid? They could destroy it. Or they could hit it with a spacecraft. The crash would change the asteroid's direction.

Not all spacecraft carry people. People on Earth **steer** them. In the future, AI could help spacecraft steer themselves. This would save time. People could work on other things.

Robots and rovers could help astronauts live on Mars. Someday, AI might even discover life on other planets!

DID YOU KNOW?

Space junk orbits Earth. This includes pieces from rockets. AI could track this trash. Tracking would help spacecraft avoid crashes. AI could aim lasers at the trash. It could steer trash away from spacecraft.

CHAPTER 3

ACTIVITIES & TOOLS

TRY THIS!

BLAST AN ASTEROID

How could you keep an asteroid from hitting Earth? Find out with this fun activity!

What You Need:
- 1 friend
- 2 ping-pong balls
- chalk

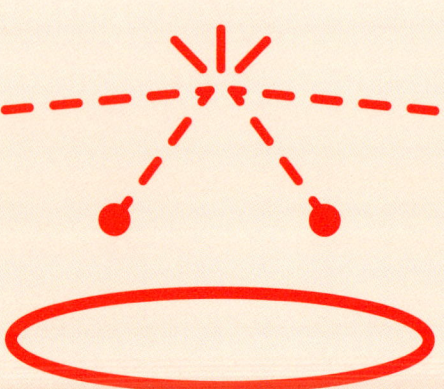

1. Go outside.
2. Draw a large circle with chalk. This circle is Earth.
3. One ball is the asteroid. Have your friend toss the ball toward the circle.
4. Using the other ball, try to hit the asteroid so it does not hit Earth.
5. Take turns. Try standing in different places. Throw the balls in different ways. Does anything make it harder to knock the asteroid away? Does anything make it easier? How is this similar or different to real asteroids?

GLOSSARY

artificial intelligence: The science of making computers do things that previously needed human intelligence, such as understanding language.

asteroid: A rocky object that travels through space.

astronauts: People trained to go to space.

craters: Large holes in the ground made by something crashing into it.

data: Information collected so something can be done with it.

laser: A device that makes a very narrow and intense beam of light.

light-years: Measures of distance in space. One light-year is 5.9 trillion miles (9.5 trillion kilometers).

orbits: Travels in a circular path around something.

robot: A machine that is programmed to perform complex human tasks.

rover: A wheeled machine that explores planets and other space objects.

sensors: Tools that notice and measure changes for a device.

spacecraft: A vehicle that travels or is used in space.

steer: To guide or direct.

INDEX

asteroid 18
astronauts 11, 12, 17, 21
cameras 6, 7
computer 6
craters 15
data 8
Earth 11, 12, 18, 21
laser 5, 7, 21
life 8, 10, 21
Mars 4, 8, 15, 21
Moon 10
robot 4, 7, 12, 17, 21
rock 5, 6, 8
rover 4, 5, 6, 7, 8, 16, 21
sensors 6, 7
spacecraft 11, 12, 17, 18, 21
space junk 21
space station 11, 12
steer 21
studies 4, 5, 6, 8, 15
universe 8, 10
water 8

TO LEARN MORE

Finding more information is as easy as 1, 2, 3.
1. Go to www.factsurfer.com
2. Enter "Alinspace" into the search box.
3. Choose your book to see a list of websites.